PURE PAGAN

PURE PAGAN

SEVEN CENTURIES OF
GREEK POEMS AND FRAGMENTS

Selected and Translated by Burton Raffel

Introduction by Guy Davenport

THE MODERN LIBRARY

NEW YORK

2004 Modern Library Edition

Translation and preface copyright © 2004 by Burton Raffel
Introduction copyright © 2004 by Guy Davenport

The map on page xxviii originally appeared on the obverse of the contents page in
The Legacy of Greece: A New Appraisal, edited by M. I. Finley (1981), in slightly differ-
ent form and is reprinted here by permission of Oxford University Press (U.K.).

LIBRARY OF CONGRESS CATALOGING-IN-PUBLICATION DATA

Pure pagan : seven centuries of Greek poems and fragments / selected and
translated by Burton Raffel; introduction by Guy Davenport.
p. cm.
ISBN 0-679-64297-8
1. Greek poetry—Translations into English. 2. Greece—Poetry. I. Raffel, Burton.

PA3622R38 2004
881'.0108—dc22   2003070646

Modern Library website address: www.modernlibrary.com

Printed in the United States of America on acid-free paper

2   4   6   8   9   7   5   3

FOR GILES ANDERSON

CONTENTS

INTRODUCTION

Guy Davenport

Burton Raffel calls these Greek poems "pagan" because they were not written in Chicago or Aberdeen. *Pagan* is defined by Samuel Johnson as meaning "heathenish"; both words, *pagan* and *heathen,* mean "living in the country." The Greeks, like all civilized people, felt that country life was more authentic, more earthy and forthright, sexier and healthier, than life in the city. It was more *natural.* So these poems are pagan because the past is another country. The pagan is always other, over yonder, or way back when, interesting because different.

Ronald Tolkien, who could speak Elvish and West Saxon, gave up the study of Greek because it was so orderly, logical, and articulate. He turned to the languages of the European North that smelled of bogs and mists. The Greek alphabet was the first clean-cut, sharply efficient graphing of sound, a fact Anne Carson celebrates in her *Eros the Bittersweet.* The old Semitic languages Phoenician and Hebrew omitted vowels; Egyptian glyphs were of whole syllables, like Arabic. Greek, as far as we know, was first written in syllabic units in Crete and Mycenae, in the clay-tablet script called Linear B by archaeologists. The alphabetizing Greeks still thought of words as syllabic units that could be joined any number of ways: *philos,* a lover; *sophos,* wise; *philosophos,* a lover of wisdom.

Written Greek was therefore a technological advance to where we are now. *Literacy* means the ability to look at patterns of letters and pronounce them—for ancient Greeks, to memorize them.

The earliest Greek poems are most certainly *songs.* Homer was sung; Sappho's and Archilochus's poems were all songs, to what kind of music we can't even guess. The plays were what we would have to call opera. Given the kinship of the ancient lyre, or *barbitos,* to the auto-harp, Sappho's cunningly woven assonances and consonances proba-bly sounded like Mother Maybelle Carter. Modern attempts to read what sparse Greek musical annotation we have, as at the first modern Olympic Games in 1896, sound perfectly awful and couldn't possibly be right.

The choruses in Greek drama were *danced* as well as sung. This should give us a clue as to their liveliness. Any Greek poem is likely to have been a song sung to a flute or lyre at a dinner party. In time, it is probable that poems became witty and convivial recitation, an art of elocution valued as a social skill. Plutarch sent the servants away to the kitchen as his *symposia* (banquets) got drunker and drunker and the recited poems became naughtier and naughtier.

Certainly Anacreon's and Meleager's homoerotic poems were re-cited at all-male dinner parties. Greek dinners were eaten on the floor by reclining guests leaning on their left arms, eating with the fingers of their right. As the common wine cup went round (Plutarch records) the diners drifted into being closer and closer to each other, just as at the theater, where there were no armrest divisions between seats, emotion (as when Oedipus blinds himself) flowed from shoulder to shoulder.

In the *Anthology*—the Greeks' own collection of their short poems, begun by Meleager around 100 B.C., expanded by Philip of Thessa-lonika in A.D. 40, and further expanded by Strato in the second century and by Agathias in the sixth, bringing the total to four thousand poems—the dominant form is that of the epigram, or inscription. Bases of statues, tombstones, and monuments have limited space; hence the perfection of the epigram as a precision of words.

The greatest of Greek inscriptions is at Thermopylae, where in 480 B.C. three hundred Spartans and their leader, Leonidas, all died holding the pass so that the rest of the Greek army could retreat from the invading Persians.

> Traveler, when you get to Sparta,
> Tell them we are still here.

This is by Simonides, a master of poignant inscriptions. (The Greek says, literally, "O stranger, this message to Lakedaimon take: we lie here obeying their orders.") Simonides (born 556 B.C.) honors the Spartans' style of brevity (the Greek is eleven words) as well as their insouciant (but boasting) heroism.

The epigrams in the *Anthology* can be sorted into the elegiac (tombstone inscriptions, memorials to the virtuous dead), the witty (satires and ironic observations of moral lapses), the silly (riddles and jokes), the erotic (beautiful boys, beautiful girls), and the drab (museum guides, statue by statue, painting by painting). The erotic poems are interesting for their anxiety about time and mortality, the brevity of human beauty. Theirs was a world without dentists, surgeons, or a medical science that went much beyond herbal remedies and recommended diets. The young body in perfect health and athletic splendor was therefore precious and desirable. The Greeks are unique in not mutilating the body in any way: They did not circumcise, pierce, tattoo (the Greek for which is *stigmata*), elongate the skull (like Egyptians and Africans), or in anywise tamper with the natural body. They did not shave (like Romans), though prostitutes depilated their pubic hair.

A tombstone for a mother of five records that her sons taught her to read and write. This touchingly says practically everything about the status of women. It is a common misunderstanding, however, to believe that women were excluded from the Olympic Games. The week before the Games in Honor of Olympian Zeus at Elis, from which women were excluded (except for the High Priestess of Eleusis), there were the Games in Honor of Olympian Hera, from which men were excluded (except for the High Priest of Zeus). These girls' games need more study. There's no mention of girls at the *gymnasion,* that social center for males. We know that in Sparta boys and girls exercised together naked, but this seems to be the exception among the Hellenic city-states.

Virginity was strictly enforced, for genealogical reasons. Plutarch patiently explained to his teenage sons and their friends that—as one of them was—being in love with a girl was normal. Greek pederasty ("desiring boys") is probably a survival of Neolithic ethics, when men were away hunting. Sons but never daughters went along on the hunt. The love affairs that occurred in camps between horny uncles and beautiful nephews became an acceptable paradigm (Zeus had his Ganymede, and Herakles his Hylas) for sergeants and recruits in the army, coaches and athletes, teachers and pupils. Being the beloved was dicey, however, as passivity in sex was effeminate. The erotic epigrams are therefore little comedies about reluctant boys.

Greece was never a country, and to talk about "the Greeks" as if they were one people is inaccurate. What they had in common was a language in many dialects. Euripides called the moon *selene;* Sappho, *selanna.* Alexander's armies spread Greek from India to Egypt. Merchants used it as a common-market tongue. Young Romans went to college in Athens to learn it, and the Roman emperor Marcus Aurelius wrote his philosophy book in it. Four anonymous biographers to whom the early church assigned the pseudonyms Matthaios, Marcus, Loukas, and Johannes wrote their Gospels in it. The library at Alexandria translated the Hebrew Scriptures into Greek. The first Christians, anxious to be different, invented *books* (pages written on both sides and bound between covers), replacing Hebrew and Greek scrolls, so the book itself is a Greek artifact. Paul preached in Greek.

The "Dark Ages" were the years in which the Latin of the Roman occupation was evolving into French, Spanish, Italian, and Romanian. A monk here and a monk there could still read Greek, but for the most part it was lost in the Catholic West, which associated it with the Orthodox Eastern schism. The Catholic Bible was in the Latin translation of Saint Jerome.

We can see the Latin West becoming curious about the Greek East as early as the twelfth century. Arab scholars (who were interesting because of their superior knowledge of astrology and medicine) knew of Greek philosophers named Al Falasafa and Aflaton: Aristotle and Plato. Robert Grosseteste and other scholars at Oxford began to study what they could find of these *authorities*—for authority commanded respect in the medieval mind.

Thus began the long exploration of Greek culture that is still continuing. The first strategic enterprise was to correct texts that had been copied by hand over the centuries, sometimes by monks ignorant of Greek. The first printers hired scholars such as Erasmus as editors and proofreaders. Oxford and Cambridge existed to provide the church with a Greek-reading clergy. A Classical Greek aesthetic pervaded architecture in eighteenth-century France, Germany, England, and the United States. The Romantic poets invented an ideal, imaginary Greece. French drama adhered to the Aristotelian unities of time and place (which Shakespeare had never heard of).

Just when we thought we knew ancient Greece, nineteenth-century archaeology began to excavate a deeper past than had been suspected. It was discovered that Egyptian mummies were sometimes wrapped in scrap paper that had once been papyrus scrolls with writing on them, and that educated Egyptians were buried with their libraries. A scroll of the poet Alkman's hymns to Hera and to Artemis (sung by choirs of Spartan girls at festivals) was discovered this way— it's on display in the Louvre. For a century now the city dump at Oxyrhynchos (a suburb of Alexandria) has been explored for the many thousands of papyrus shreds it contains: fragments of Gospels,

Sappho, Archilochus, personal letters, grocery lists. Add to these discoveries the Greek habit of using broken pottery to write on. One of Sappho's most beautiful songs survives on one of these *ostraka*. These ceramic shards were also used as ballots; hence our word *ostracize,* "to vote out of office."

Greek lyric poetry is therefore the latest specimen of their literature to emerge, and counts as a salient inspiration for modern poetry. It can be discerned easily in *Spoon River Anthology* (1915), Edgar Lee Masters's conscious imitation of the epitaphs in the Greek *Anthology,* in Hilda Doolittle ("H.D."), in Ezra Pound, William Carlos Williams, Kenneth Rexroth, and even T. S. Eliot, whose "Sweeney Erect" begins with an imitation of Anacreon.

A vast amount of Greek poetry survives in prose texts; Plato and Plutarch were habitual quoters. Grammarians, too. But for the most part, Greek poetry is lost to us forever. What has been recovered is all the more valuable.

The *Iliad* and the *Odyssey* are noble; the plays of Euripides, Aeschylus, and Sophocles still define tragedy; Aristophanes and Menander define comedy. In the lyric poets we have charmingly defined examples of an ancient sensibility that's both domestic and public. The Greek word that means "the content of a culture" is *paideuma* (from the word *pais,* "child"), what you know just by being a Greek, a Dogon, an Icelander. All the tacit assumptions of daily life constitute *paideuma.* So poets compose for an audience that understands them. This dimension of difference is what Burton Raffel is calling "pagan." Difference creates information; that is, the crossover from what we know to what we don't.

A local travel article recently advised against a visit to the Florentine Academy, where Michelangelo's *David* stands, as this superb statue is "embarrassing." It's embarrassing to American families because of its nudity. The gospel of Matthew begins, "The booke of the generation of Iesus Christ, the sonne of Dauid,..." and continues for the rest of the page tracing the forty-one generations from Abraham to Jesus. The genitalia Michelangelo realistically sculpted was understood in 1504 to be theologically significant by the pious, and aesthetically significant to the humanists who appreciated the statue's derivation from Greek art. David's being naked is a poignant heroic symbol in that *gymnos* ("naked") principally meant "without armor." David slew an armored giant with his slingshot.

So contemporary prudery has trouble with Greek nudity. If you were at the theater in Athens (it's still there, and worth a visit), the play did not begin until the god Dionysos had been led in—to a glory of silver trumpets and drumrolls. He took the form of a white bull wearing a garland around his neck. He was led in—all stand!—by two Olympic athletes, as naked as they were born and as naked as when they won their crowns of wild olive in the Games in Honor of Olympian Zeus at Elis. Dionysos stood in a marble stall between the High Priestess of Demeter, on his right, and the Archon of Athens, on his left. Then the orchestra (lyres, flutes, drums) struck up the overture and onto the stage came an actor in high-heeled boots and wearing the mask of King Oedipus, led (he is blind) by his daughter Antigone, singing words written for him by Sophocles:

> Teknon typhlou gerontos, Antigone, tinas
> khorous aphigmeth' e tinon andron polin;

"Antigone, child of a blind old man, where are we, what city have we come to?" The audience is proud and thrilled. They know where he is—in a sacred grove called Kolonos, just down the road from where they sit in their theater. Over their shoulders they can see the newly finished Parthenon, most beautiful of buildings, a temple to the city's guardian deity, Athena, goddess of skill and the intellect. This blind old king has come from Myth, from the deep past, when things were with him out of measure all his life. He has come to a city where (as

Yeats translated) "body is not bruised to pleasure soul." Antigone describes what she can see to her blind father: the Athenian Acropolis where this play is being performed.

They did things with style, *their* style. When *Oedipus at Kolonos* was first performed, the poet had been three years dead (at age ninety-one). The air was full of a sense of *honor,* a sentiment we recognize, at least. Add *splendor* (the trumpets, athletes, Dionysos incarnate). We don't think of the theater as religious, nor the Olympics. The athletes are for us the nexus of two felonies, indecent exposure on their part, voyeurism on ours. Burton Raffel's *pagan* becomes eloquent when we see how many of our taboos the ancient Greeks thought natural and civilized.

Cultural mentalities are more often than not exclusive and inscrutable. Down through history, however, one culture or another proved to be attractive and desirable. The Romans imported Greek art and architecture; they admired and emulated Greek poetry and philosophy; they even pretended that they shared the same gods, equating, for example, their archaic owl goddess Minerva with the Greek Pallas Athene. This syncretism had begun with the Greeks themselves, when they matched up their pantheon with that of Egypt.

Greek culture is therefore familiar to us through an ancestral family resemblance. We inherited their alphabet, and in the Renaissance we used their language for science and medicine. The English language was shaped by Danish Vikings trying to talk to Angles and Saxons. In 1066 Norman French was added to the mixture (itself being an evolved Latin dialect). We still say "last will and testament," along with many other legal terms that accommodate both English and French ears. The law was in Latin; science was in Greek. *Proton, neutron, electricity, oxygen, diarrhea, apnea, hypotenuse, polygon, pneumonia, psychosis*—these are all Greek words.

Translators into English have four vocabularies at their disposal: archaic Dano-Saxon, French, Latin, and Greek. Burton Raffel uses basic English, mainly, understanding that he's working with plain Greek. No word in another language exactly fits an English word. I recently did a translation of the sayings of Jesus in which John the Baptist turns up as John the Dipper. That's what Greek ears heard: a man named John who dipped people in a river.

Not all Greek words have an equivalent in English. In a poem of Theocritus a goat is eating something. Look up what he's eating in a Greek-English dictionary. The definition is "a plant eaten by a goat in Theocritus." In a beautiful hymn to Aphrodite we aren't certain whether the goddess is sitting on an intricately carved throne or wearing an elaborately embroidered dress.

Philological problems can be solved; the problems of distant sentiments remain. Pathos, humor, sarcasm, appetence, grief, satire: these spin differently in other cultures. When Priapos, the fertility god, is sporting an erection, is he comic, erotic, worshipful, or grotesque? Some sentiments are universal. "Help him out of the boat, Charon," reads an epitaph, "he's wearing his first pair of shoes."

Human nature is of a wholeness. We are animals who can talk. We aren't as sane as we might be. Our distinction is that we changed from being wild to being (as Aristotle said) companionable, social, and civilized. Around the Parthenon the frieze showed people and horses. This, to the Greek eye, was symbolic. Horses have to be tamed. Man is the animal that tamed himself. Greek philosophy and literature was all in the service of civilizing, of understanding human nature, of questioning and sharpening our ethics, our sense of beauty, our ability to appreciate and honor the world. The first word of the Greeks' greatest poem, the epic *Iliad*, is *menin*, "anger"—the anger of Achilles that was furious, destructive, insane. The last word of the *Iliad* is *hippodamoio*, "horse tamer." *Thus was the funeral of Hektor the tamer of horses.* From Homer to the Parthenon frieze is seven hundred, plausibly a thousand years. Both the Parthenon and Homer see civilization as a process of taming, of civilizing. The West has two sources, seemingly inexhaustible: the Hebrew dialogue with God and the Greek dialogue of mankind with itself, of which Greek poetry is a charmingly human part.

———

GUY DAVENPORT is professor emeritus of English at the University of Kentucky. His best-known book is *The Geography of the Imagination* and his most recent *The Death of Picasso*. He is the author of ten books of critical commentary, nine of short fiction, and seven of translations of Greek texts. He is also a painter and illustrator. He lives in Lexington, Kentucky.

Translator's Preface

We have come to know Homer well, in this Greekless age. We know Aeschylus and Sophocles and Euripides; we know Aristophanes; we know Sappho and even Archilochus. Shorter (lyric) Greek poetry before the Christian era has also been remarkably well preserved, considering the accidents of time and the malice of authority. Yet with a few isolated exceptions we do not know (or even encounter) Alkaios or Alkman, Anyte or Callimachus, Meleager or Simonides. And those other, nameless wonders of Greek poetry that have come down to us through the centuries, now necessarily piled in a generic heap and ascribed to the universal authorship of "Anonymous," are even less known, though often no less piercingly beautiful, no less witty or wise.

For there is indeed something we can call the spirit of ancient Greece, a carefully tuned voice that speaks out of the grave with astonishing clarity and grace, a distinctive voice that, taken as a whole, is like no other voice that has ever sung on this earth. We know a great deal of ancient Greece when we know Homer; we know a great deal when we know the tragedians and Aristophanes, when we know Sappho and Archilochus. But the picture is incomplete, sometimes sadly incomplete, unless we also have some awareness of the sharp, keen bursts of song that are represented in the pages that follow.

There are many poets who have drunk and studied at this fount; some such poets still exist in our time, notably the magnificent C. P. Cavafy. It is not, I think, platitudinous to suggest that ancient Greek lyric poetry is virtually an inexhaustible resource, one that contemporary writers can always resort to with plain profit both for themselves and for their readers. I would myself classify most of the poetry in this book as more quintessentially "modern" than most of what you will find in our contemporary literary periodicals. That, I would maintain, is neither a platitude nor a conundrum. To see why, simply read the poems: they have better answers than I do.

Most of what has survived is from written (manuscript) sources, some fragmentary, some put together in collections or anthologies. (Printing had, of course, not been invented until long after the final entry in the Greek *Anthology* had been recorded.) But we must remember that the material on which things were written was emphatically *not* the paper we know today, most of which comes from wood pulp and ages and self-destructs rapidly. Indeed, the materials used then were not even paper made from rags, as most paper was before the early nineteenth century. Most of these ancient Greek poems were transcribed either on what is called parchment (specially prepared animal skins) or on papyrus (reeds—primarily from Egypt—pressed and dried into a tough flat stuff eminently suitable for writing purposes). These survive, obviously, far longer than ordinary modern paper.

In fact, since the processes involved in the production of these writing materials were relatively expensive, for centuries people have tried to maximize them—we might say, make them more cost-efficient. They were extensively used (for example, in mummy casings). And when book binding began, and paperlike materials were needed to bind *new* books, craftsmen took *old* manuscripts and used them for what they thought was one last go-round. But an investigator in Vienna, Dr. Anton Fackelmann, has been damp-steaming mummy cases and old book bindings to try to recover even more ancient writings. He has been outstandingly successful: the closest thing we have ever had to a complete poem by Archilochus (seventh century B.C.), for example, was thus discovered. Others are busy doing much the same sort of thing.

I have not attempted to make historical sense of this largely fragmentary and somewhat haphazardly preserved mass of song. When so few people still know, today, what the dates and the sparse, fragmented biographical details mean, dates and biographies seem to me largely irrelevant. And even presented in simple, arbitrary, alphabetical order, with invented titles (ancient poems almost never bore titles) that are also grouped alphabetically, this seems to me a poetic corpus that can be left to define itself.

My decision to translate only less well known poems and poets is both deliberate and not in any sense a seeking after novelty. Rather, it is a conscious attempt to avoid duplicating the truly splendid translations of people like Dudley Fitts, Guy Davenport, and Mary Barnard. When one supremely viable translation exists, I see no reason to fashion another one.

I have not embroidered any of the poems, though I have not even tried to mangle poetry by translating "literally." I respect these poems, and these poets, far too deeply to destroy them by so-called literal translation, or by attempting to reproduce the linguistic unreproducibles of meter and form. But these remain translations, not imitations. I have tried to let the ancient poets speak through me. I have also tried as hard as I am able not to put words into their mouths.

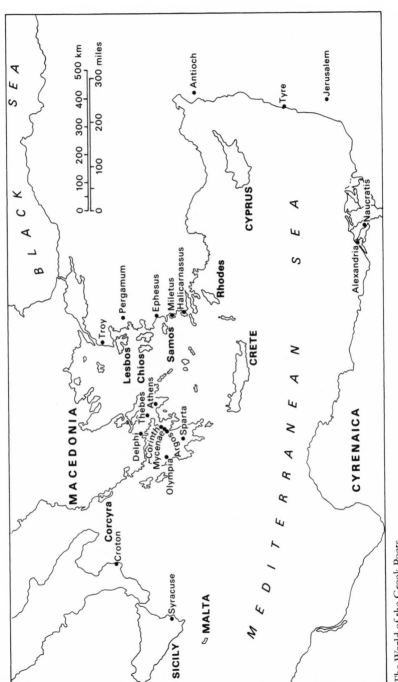

The World of the Greek Poets

PURE PAGAN

ALKAIOS

AGRICULTURE

Trees:
All right,
Plant trees.
But first
Plant
Vines.

BACCHUS

Give up? How stupid,
Just for bad luck!
Nothing will work.
But Bacchus, Bacchus, if we forget your name
In our weariness, wine is the medicine
To call for, the best medicine
To drink deep, deep.

COURAGE

When courage is what he needs
He finds it in himself.

DRINK, AND GET DRUNK WITH ME

Melanippus: drink, and get drunk with me.
Once you've crossed the swirling Acheron
And landed in darkness, what makes you think
You'll ever see sunlight again?
Don't be a fool—don't try too hard.
King Sisyphus, son of Aeolus, was the smartest man alive
And thought he could run from death,
But Fate drove him across the Acheron, then drove him over again,
And the king of darkness, Cronos' son,
Set him a miserable task down under the black earth.
Don't even hope for such things.

DRINKING

Drink. Why wait for the lamps?
There's only a finger of daylight left.
Get the big cups, the ones with pictures.
Bacchus gave us wine to drown our sorrows.
Mix one of water to two of wine,
Fill them to the brim,
And let one cup quickly follow the other.

FRANKNESS

Speak
As you please
And hear
What can never
Please.

FRIENDSHIP

Friends? My friends are nothing,
And I weep for them,
And for me.

HISTORY

Not us: no.
It began with our fathers,
I've heard.

LOVE

I loathe Love, wasting his arrows on me
Instead of aiming at huge wild beasts.
Do gods win glory by burning up men?
Is my head a noble trophy to hang from his belt?

MOURNING

Wine, now, and more wine, and more,
And more,
Now that Myrsillus is dead.

MOVERS AND SHAKERS

If a man shakes loose stones
To make a wall with,
Stones may fall on his head
Instead.

PARVENU

Even if he came from somewhere else,
You would say you did, too.

PATIENCE

Drink: the Dog Star
Is coming back, so
Drink.

PHILOSOPHY

Nothing
Will
Come
Of
Anything.

PIGGERY

Again
Again
Pigs whip up

            muck
            mud
            slop

Again.

POLITICS

He wants power
He has power
He wants more
And his country will break in his hands,
Is breaking now.

POVERTY

Poverty:
Miserable,
Powerful,
O Poverty, you and your sister Helplessness
Fall like wolves
On this country
Once so great.

SOCIAL RELATIONS

I had you to dinner, once,
Gave you tender goat, juicy pork:
How to win friends
And influence people.

SORROW

Sorrow:
You've made me completely forget sorrow.

TRUE LUXURY

And the sky god pours down rain,
And the clouds whirl, and rivers freeze:
So: keep your fire high
And pour out honey-sweet wine
And lie back
With a pillow on this side,
And a pillow on that side.

TRUTH

Boy:
Boy:
Wine

And

Truth.

WINE

Wine
Opens
Keyholes
Wide.

ALKMAN

FATE AND NECESSITY

The thread
Runs thin,
The need
Runs hard,
Hard.

GLUTTONOUS ALKMAN

And a huge cauldron, hot
With your dinner, soon.
But still cold, until that thick winter soup
For gluttonous Alkman
Comes boiling up.
No fancy slop for Alkman, no.
Like ordinary people he likes real food.

NOT APHRODITE, NO

Not Aphrodite, no. But like a child,
Wild, Love comes down,
Almost as though walking on flowers—
But should not touch them,
Should not,
No.

O DANCERS

O dancers, singers, honey-voiced girls,
Loud, clear: no more, I cannot!
God, O God, if I were only a kingfisher,
Purple like the sea, flying never afraid
Out over the waves
Forever.

SET SEVEN COUCHES

Set seven couches
And seven tables
And cover them with poppy cakes,
And linseed cakes,
And sesame cakes,
In and among the wooden bowls.

TANTALUS

Tantalus, Evil placed in the middle of Good,
Sat under a hanging rock, ready to fall,
And thought he saw,
And saw

Nothing.

THE PEAKS ARE ASLEEP

The peaks
                              are asleep
And gulleys
And ravines
                              are asleep
And creeping things
Out of the dark earth
And the beasts on the hills
                              are asleep
And bees, all bees
And monsters deep in the sea
                              are asleep
And asleep, too, every flying bird everywhere
                         asleep.

TRY SINGING

For feasts
For feasting
For eating with men
Try singing as you eat.

ANONYMOUS

A MIRROR

Look: I look back. You look with eyes
But I am eyeless.
And I can speak, having no voice. You have
A voice, but all I have is lips, and they move, soundless.

AN EPITAPH

I was Callicrita, I bore twenty-nine children
And all of them lived, and still live.
I died at a hundred and five
And never needed a cane to steady my hand.

AN ORACLE

This isthmus: no digging, no fencing.
If Zeus had wanted an island he'd have made one.

ARISTO

He lived by his sling,
Hunting winged geese,
Creeping silently up
As they fed, watching on every side
But not seeing him.
He lived poor, he died poor.
Now he lives in the darkness
And his sling hangs motionless,
No hand to whirl it
Swift and sure,
And the geese fly over his tomb.

EARTHQUAKE

Once corpses left the city behind them, dead,
But now the living carry the city to her grave.

EPIGRAM

Take what you have while you have it: you'll lose it soon enough.
A single summer turns a kid into a shaggy goat.

EPITAPH

Seafarer, don't bother about my name.
Pray for a kinder sea.

LOVERS' DIALOGUE

He: Hello, pretty one.

She: Hello.

He: Who walks ahead of you?

She: None of your business.

He: But I have business in mind.

She: My mistress.

He: Is there any hope?

She: For what?

He: One night.

She: How much can you pay her?

He: Gold.

She: There's hope.

He: Here's what I have.

She: That's all? Forget it.
           She charges more for hope.

MESSAGE TO THE LIVING

I'm dead, but waiting for you, and you'll wait for someone:
The darkness waits for everyone, it makes no distinctions.

MIRACLE

Here I lie, beneath this stone, the famous woman
Who untied her belt for only one man.

ON BEING OLD

I was young,
I was poor.
Now I'm old
And I'm rich.
Only I of all men living
Have been miserable
In youth and in age.
I could have used riches
When I had none,
And now I have them
And what can I use them for?

ON HOMER

Let Homer be worshiped as a god, if he is a god.
But if not a god, let him appear godlike all the same.

ON LOVE

Venus, who saves sailors: save me,
Dear goddess, who die, shipwrecked, here on dry land.

PATRIOTS

Spring makes leaves,
Leaves make the earth lovely
Just as stars make the heavens shine,
And these beautiful fields make Greece lovely,
And these brave men
Make their country wonderful.

PRAYER

Zeus, king, give us good even if we don't pray for it,
And give us nothing evil even if that is what we pray for.

ANTIPATER OF SIDON

ALKMENES

My name was Alkmenes. I drove birds
From the fields, starlings and high-flying robber cranes.
I was swinging my sling at a crowd
Of birds when a viper bit my ankle,
Injected her bitter poison in my veins,
And stole the sunlight.
See? I was watching the air
And never saw what was right on the ground in front of me.

AMYNTOR

Amyntor, Philip's son, lies in this Lydian soil.
His hands were full of iron war.
No sickness led him into the darkness:
He died holding his shield over a wounded friend.

ARES, GOD OF WAR

Who gave me these shining shields,
Hung them, unstained, on my walls?
Who gave me these unbroken helmets?
Murderous Ares needs no ornaments.
Will no one drag them out of my temple?
Give them to drunkards,
Give them to men of peace:
I have no use for tinsel and show.
I want trophies hacked by the sword,
I want the blood of dying men,
For I am Ares,
I am the Destroyer of men and weapons.

DIODORUS

Diodorus, son of Calligenes of Olynthus,
Diodorus, who could take a ship as far as Atlas
And knew the waters of Crete
And could sail the Black Sea,
Diodorus died in port,
Dropping into the waves
As he leaned over the bow
And threw up what he'd eaten and drunk.
How shallow a depth of water
Drowned him, he who had conquered
All the wide oceans!

Antipater of Thessalonika

A QUARREL

The ship broke apart
And two men fought in the water,
Fighting for a wooden beam.
Antagorus hit Pisistratus.
It was no crime,
For his life was at stake,
But Justice saw and frowned.
So Pisistratus swam to safety
And Antagorus was swallowed by a shark.
Justice is always Justice,
Even out on the ocean.

EUROPA

Europa costs you a dollar. No one cares,
Including her. She's got clean sheets
And a fire in winter. Why bother
Becoming a bull, O Zeus!

POETIC GIFT

Antipater sends you a birthday poem,
Piso, a poem he wrote in one night.
Take it to your heart
And praise its maker,
As Zeus is won
By a gift of perfume.

ANYTE

EPITAPH FOR A SLAVE

He was a slave, alive.
Dead, he's as great as mighty Darius.

HERMES

Here I stand
At the crossroads,
Next to the windswept trees,
Near the gray cold beach.
I offer tired travelers rest.
The water I offer
Is cold and pure.

STRANGER

Stranger, weary from much walking: rest under this elm,
Hear the sweet breeze in its green leaves,
Drink cold water from this fountain: here
Is where travelers always rest, in our burning heat.

VENUS

This is Venus' place,
For she loves to smile at the bright sea
And make sailors happy.
All around her the sea trembles,
Seeing her loveliness.

ARATUS

IN THE BEGINNING

Begin with Zeus, on every man's lips.
The streets are full of Zeus, and all the marketplaces;
The sea is full of Him, and the harbors:
All of us need Zeus everywhere we go.
For Zeus has fathered us all, and smiles on us,
And shows us his kindness, and sends us off to our work,
Reminding us what must be done.
He tells us when to yoke up oxen,
When to hoe, when to sow seed, and what to plant.
For it was Zeus who gave us the heavens
And divided the sky into stars,
And shaped each star differently,
And then made each star point to a season
So men could read His heavens and understand,
And all things could grow as they should.
We pray to Him first, we pray to Him last:

Hail, Father, wonder-worker, men's great blessing,
Hail to You and to those who came before You.
And hail, gentle Muses, smiling on men:
Guide my song, help me,
For I bow to you and pray.

ASCLEPIADES

DRY FRUIT

My arms hold Archansa, a shriveled old whore
Whose wrinkles were once love's sweetness.
O lovers who picked her young blossoms, piercing fresh, brilliant,
What a fiery furnace you came through!

PYTHIAS

Remember, O Night, how tricky Pythias
Plays her usual games. I came
When she called me; she called me, and I came. Just once
Let her stand at my door and cry as I'm crying.

RENDEZVOUS

Nico, famous Nico, swore by solemn Demeter
She'd come tonight. But the night's half gone
And where is she? Could she have lied, and to me?
Slaves: blow out the lights.

CALLIMACHUS

AN EPITAPH

He was a stranger; he did not stay here long;
He needs no long-winded story.
"Here lies a man of Crete, Theris, Aristos' son."
But how long a story for me!

CHARIDAS

A: Stone: do you stand on the grave of Charidas?

B: The son of Arimmas of Cyrene?
He lies here.

A: Charidas: what's it like down there?

C: Dark, all dark.

A: And do the dead come back?

C: Lies, all lies.

A: And Pluto?

C: A myth, no more.

A: I've no hope left.

C: I speak the truth.
But I can tell you good news, too:
Meat is cheap, down here.

CRITAS' TOMB

If you go to the north, you'll find
Hippacus and Dido with no trouble. Their family is famous.
Give them my painful message: tell them I stand
Covering Critas' tomb, Critas, their beloved son.

GROUSE

I hate poems that go on and on and on.
I hate roads where everyone walks.
I loathe wandering lovers, nor will I drink from just any well.
I detest everything common.
Oh, you're handsome, Lysus, you're very handsome.
But even as Echo says it again, I hear: "He belongs to someone else."

MY HUNTER LOVE

Hunters in the hills track down every rabbit,
Every deer, running through the snow.
Show them a wounded animal
And they leave it where it lies.
Just so my love: it hunts whatever runs
And ignores what lies waiting.

MY MIND

All the shining perfumes I splashed on my head,
And all the fragrant flowers I wore,
Soon lost their scent.
Everything I put between my teeth
And dropped into my ungrateful belly
Was gone by morning.
The only things I can keep
Came in through my ears.

STEPMOTHERS

A boy bent to drape flowers on his stepmother's grave,
Thinking that death had changed her,
But the stone toppled and killed him.
Stepsons! Be wary even when they're dead!

THE STATUE OF APOLLO AT DELOS

"Are you the Delian Apollo?"

"I am."

"Are you thirty feet high?"

"By the god I am, I am."

"All of gold?"

"All of gold."

"And naked?"

"Wearing only a belt."

"And why do the goddesses of beauty and charm stand in your right hand, while you keep your great bow in your left?"

"My bow aims at fools. It keeps them from arrogance. But I offer beauty to the good, and I offer it freely."

THE UNKNOWN'S TOMB

Who are you, shipwrecked stranger? Leontias found you,
Dead on this beach, and buried you,
Weeping for his own uncertain life, for he too skims
The waves like a gull, and never rests.

WINNING AND LOSING

The winning poet is brief.
"I won," he says. No more.
But ask the losing poet.
"Oh, it's a damned hard business!" he cries.
Zeus: let the miserable wail at length.
Give me shortness of breath.

DIONYSIOS OF ANDROS

AN EPITAPH

No wonder I slipped, and fell, and died,
Soaked by Zeus outside,
Soaked by Bacchus within.
The odds were two to one
And they were gods.

GLAUKOS

DAPHNIS AND PAN

A: Nymphs, O nymphs, tell me
The truth. Did Daphnis pass here,
Rest with his white goats?

B: Yes, piper Pan, yes.
He cut a message in the bark of that poplar,
A message for you.
"Pan, Pan, go to Malea,
Come to the mountain of Sophis.
You'll find me there."

A: Farewell, nymphs!

HEGEMON

THERMOPYLAE

Passing this tomb, some somber stranger
Might say: "Here the courage of a thousand Spartans
Stopped a million Persians, and died facing
The enemy. This is what Sparta means."

LEONIDAS

ON CLITO

Here is his hut, the bit of land
He planted, the thin old vines
He grew, his patch of brushwood.
But he lived here eighty years!

LEONIDAS OF TARENTUM

AN EPITAPH

Stranger, listen to Orthon of Syracuse:
"Don't go out drunk on a winter night."
I died in the snow, drunk,
And instead of resting in my own rich country
I lie forever wearing this foreign earth.

HIS OWN EPITAPH

I lie far from Italy, far from Tarentum
Where I came from. This distance is worse than death.
This is how wanderers live: it is not life.
But the Muses loved me and my sadness
Turns into sweetness. My name is not lost,
The Muses' gifts bring this dead Leonidas
Everywhere the sun still shines.

THE VINE AND THE GOAT

A bearded, bouncing billy goat
Chewed all the blossoms off a vine,
And from deep in the earth the vine spoke to him:
"Monster! Rip off my branches, destroy my fruit,
But your evil jaws can't reach my roots,
And they'll send up sweet nectar
And make a sacrificial offering
To pour into the sacred earth
When your throat's been slit by a priestly knife."

MELEAGER

DAPHNIS

I, goat-footed Pan, will no longer live
High on the hilltops.
What are mountains to me, now that Daphnis is dead?
He made a fire in my heart.
I'll live here in cities:
Let someone else
Hunt wild beasts.
Pan renounces his old life
Now that his love is dead.

HELIODORA

Heliodora's garland fades, but she glows,
Shining bright, a garland for her garland.

ON HIMSELF

I grew on Tyre,
I was born in Syria,
And I came out of Eucrates,
I, Meleager, who taught my muse
To run on barbed feet.
I'm a Syrian: should anyone be surprised?
But stranger, all of us live in one country: the world.
All of us were born in the same Chaos.
And when I grew old
I wrote this epitaph for myself,
Knowing that old age and death live side by side.
Say something to wish this wordsmith well,
And live to be a wordy old man like me.

SPRING

Winter winds have blown out of the sky;
The purple spring flowers happily.
The dark earth drapes herself in green
And plants burst into leaf, their newborn hair waving.
Fields drink the dawn dew and grow,
Laughing as roses open. Shepherds in the hills
Shrill bright melodies on their pipes,
And goatherds count and re-count their white kids.
Sailors are out on the broad sea,
Zephyr puffing out their sails.
Men wear crowns of ivy and cry "Evoe!"
To honor Bacchus, father of wine.
Bees buzz into being, stir and work their hives,
Constructing artful many-celled combs.
And all the races of birds sing everywhere,
Clear and loud: kingfishers near the water,
Swallows around our houses, swans by the river's edge,
Nightingales deep in the woods.
And if leaves and plants are happy, and the earth sprouts,
And shepherds pipe, and sheep play and dance in the meadows,
And bees make honey,
How can a poet be silent, seeing beautiful spring?

TIMO

Venus never boarded your boat,
Timo, when its timbers were new.
But now your back bends like a drooping yardarm,
Your gray sails sag, your breasts flap in the wind,
And your ship's belly wrinkles in the waves,
All sloppy with bilgewater,
Her joints gone loose.
What a voyage, sailing alive,
Not dead, over Acheron's lake
On this ancient coffin!

TO VENUS

Meleager brings you his lamp, O Venus,
For it knows how he celebrates you in the dark.

Menander

THE SOURCE OF DESTRUCTION

Child: understand me:
Everything that decays rots from the inside out,
Rots with its own corruption.
Watch rust destroying iron,
Moths eating out woven wool,
Worms chewing through wood.
But the worst rot of all is envy,
The evil root of the faithless soul—
And envy is eating you away,
It is eating at you as I speak,
And it will go on eating.

VANITY

To learn just who you are
Look at tombs as you walk.
They hold the bones, the powdered dust
Of kings and tyrants, of wise men,
Of men proud of their noble fathers,
Of men glorying in their gold and their glory
And their beautiful bodies.
And when the time came
What protected them against death?
Nothing. Everyone living dies the same death.
Look at tombs and learn just who you are.

MENECRATES

OLD AGE

We all pray for it
Before it comes,
Then blame it
When it arrives.
Old age is a debt
We like to be owed,
Not one we like to collect.

PERSES

ON PREGNANCY

Artemis: Timessa gave you her pretty dress,
And her belt, and her breast band,
When after ten months she struggled hard
And at last was free of her burden and her pain.

PHALAECUS

THE SEA AND THE LAND

If life means much to you,
And long life means more,
Stay away from the waves,
Think of the plough and the oxen that draw it.
Landsmen live to grow gray hair,
But not men who travel the sea.

PHILODEMUS

A GIRL'S SPEECH

You moan, miserable. You gawk,
You're jealous, you kiss me, you paw me.
How loverlike. And then I say: "I'm here!"
And you flop like a fish instead of a lover.

RENDEZVOUS

I came through the rain, soaked,
Dodging my husband.
And now we sit and do nothing, neither talk
Nor sleep as lovers ought to sleep.

PHOCYLIDES

THE LERIANS

Phocylides says: All Lerians are evil. Not one good,
One bad, but all of them—except Procles,
And Procles too is a Lerian.

PLATO

A CAUTIONARY TALE

He lost his gold,
And *he,* finding the first man's gold,
Lost his belt,
And then he who lost his gold
Found the other man's belt
And hanged himself.

AN EPITAPH

I am a drowned man's tomb. There is a farmer's.
Death waits for us all, whether at sea or on land.

ON LOVE

Your lover throws you an apple, Xantippe:
Please him, please: apples and women both rot.

THE ERETRIAN DEAD

We who lie here once left the Aegean's loud waves
For this silent plain.
Farewell, glorious Eretria, where we used to live.
Farewell, Athens, shining neighbor.
Farewell, O beloved sea.

TIME

Everything comes from time.
Time changes
                  names
                            shapes
                                        nature
                                                      fortune:
Everything.

POSIDIPPUS

PARTY PREPARATIONS

We'll be four, each with his woman.
Eight's too many for one keg of wine.
Go tell Aristus the keg I bought
Is only half full, a gallon short, maybe two
Or even more. Hurry!
They're coming at five.

SIMONIDES

AN EPITAPH

I, Brotachos of Crete, lie in this ground,
Where I came not to die but to buy and sell.

EPITAPH FOR A WORKMAN

No Croesus lies buried here, but a poor laborer.
This tomb is all I need, now.

HOW TO TELL

Blamed for nothing,
Able to do
Everything: this
Is how we know
A god.

ON HIS SPEAR

Rest, O my long spear, on Zeus' high column.
Stay sacred to Him.
Your blade is old: many battles
Have worn it dull.

SAILORS

These men lying here were carrying honors to Apollo.
One sea, one night, one ship carried them to their graves.

THE DEFENDERS OF TEGEA

Their bravery made sure
That no smoke from great Tegea reached the sky.
They chose to leave their children
A city blossoming with freedom
And chose death instead,
Right in the center of the battle.

TIMON

Timon of Rhodes lies here, who drank his fill,
And ate his fill, and said whatever he thought of every man he knew.

TERPANDER

OF SPARTA

Where spears and songs,
Young men's spears and sweet clear songs,
And what makes men noble, Justice,
Justice walks in the broad streets.

TO APOLLO

Sing me,
My soul, oh
Sing me the far-ranging
Lord.

TO ZEUS

Zeus, in whom all things begin,
Ruler of everything,
Zeus, to begin my hymns
I bring You this
As a gift.

THEODORIDAS

AN EPITAPH

This is a drowned man's tomb. Sail on, stranger,
For when we went down the other ships sailed on.

EUPHORION

Euphorion the exquisite poet
Lies under these harbor stones.
Offer that knowing singer a peach or an apple, or even berries,
For when he lived he loved all of them.

ABOUT THE POETS

ALKAIOS: Born about 620 B.C. Resident of Mytilene, major city on the island of Lesbos (where Sappho also lived). Deeply involved in politics, he fought unsuccessfully against the tyrant then ruling the island and fled to Egypt. He eventually returned and reconciled with the ruler. Death date unknown.

ALKMAN: Flourished 654–611 B.C. Resided in Sparta but may have been born in Lydia. He is said to have been a slave, released because of his poetic skills. Most of his work is lost.

ANTIPATER OF SIDON: Flourished about 120 B.C. No other data available.

ANTIPATER OF THESSALONIKA: Late first century B.C.; known to have been alive and writing at about A.D. 12–15. He had been associated with and earlier (11 B.C.) supported by a Roman statesman who may also have patronized the great Latin poet Horace. Horace's *Ars Poetica* may have been composed for this patron's sons.

ANYTE: Early third century B.C. Known to have translated Sappho (whose dialect was difficult for "modern" Greeks, after four hundred years). She is also known to have pioneered the making of epitaphs for animals and was among the first to write pastorally about nondomesticated nature.

ARATUS: Approximately 315–240 B.C. Known to have lived for a time in Athens, arriving there about 291 B.C.; he there met and became friendly with his younger contemporary Callimachus. He moved to the court of Macedon, about 276 B.C., and was active in the literary circle there until about 270 B.C., when political turmoil led him to remove to the court of Antiochus I. He there produced an edition of Homer's *Odyssey*. He is said to have returned to Macedon and died there.

ASCLEPIADES: About 320 B.C. From Samos. An early writer of literary epigrams, notably about love. He was a contemporary of Theocritus and was known to and attacked by Callimachus.

CALLIMACHUS: About 305–240 B.C. From Cyrene, but migrated to Alexandria, where he was first a schoolteacher and then a cataloguer for the great library there. He was the teacher of Apollonius Rhodius, with whom he later quarreled most bitterly. One of the most famous poets of his time, he was widely read, imitated, discussed—and attacked. A large amount of his work has survived.

DIONYSIOS OF ANDROS: No reliable data.

GLAUKOS: No reliable data.

HEGEMON: Probably fourth century B.C. Parodist from Thasos. He won many prizes in Athens and was known to Aristotle.

LEONIDAS: First century A.D.? Known to have lived in Alexandria. An astrologer first and then a poet, he wrote numerological poems of great arithmetic complexity.

LEONIDAS OF TARENTUM: First half of the third century B.C. Apparently led a wandering life. He was famous for his epigrams, which were often deeply pessimistic.

MELEAGER: Flourished 100 B.C. Born in Syria, lived in Tyre. Trilingual, he spoke Greek, Syrian, and Phoenician. He wrote epigrams, often influenced by earlier poets (whose work he collected in his *Garland,* an anthology).

MENANDER: 342/341 B.C. to 293/289 B.C. From Athens. Comedic playwright of high reputation.

MENECRATES: Born about 340 B.C. From Epheseus. He wrote didactic poetry, now lost, and a poem on agriculture, also lost.

PERSES: Late fourth century B.C. From Thebes.

PHALAECUS: No reliable data.

PHILODEMUS: About 110 B.C. to 40/35 B.C. Resident in Rome after about 75 B.C. He was a philosopher and writer of epigrams, mostly about love, often risqué. His prose writing is mostly lost. He seems to have been a teacher of Horace.

PHOCYLIDES: Mid–sixth century B.C.; flourished 544–541. From Miletus. Much of his surviving work is gnomic.

PLATO: About 429–347 B.C. Athenian philosopher and, early on, writer of elegiac love poems, of considerable importance in the development of that form. When his teacher, Socrates, was executed in 399 B.C., Plato retired to Megara, then did a great deal of traveling. About 387, he returned to Athens and, almost at once, founded the famous Academy. He taught there for the remainder of his life. His most famous student, Aristotle, arrived at the Academy in 367 B.C. and stayed until Plato died.

POSIDIPPUS: Flourished 270 B.C. From Samos. His surviving poetry is distinctly sexual.

SIMONIDES: About 556–468 B.C. From Iulis in Ceos. Both a lyric and an elegiac poet, he lived for a considerable time in Athens. He was widely traveled and wrote much about people and events there and throughout Greece, including the Spartan role in the battle of Thermopylae, the battle of Marathon, and the Greek victory at Artemisium. Plutarch describes him as physically a very ugly man; Aristotle records that after declining to write a poem, he was offered a higher fee and then accepted the commission. He died in Syracuse, where he spent roughly the last decade of his life. Most of his poetry has been lost.

TERPANDER: Mid–seventh century B.C. From Lesbos. He was highly successful as both poet and musician, and may have founded a school of music in Sparta. Most of his work is lost; details of his life are minimal.

THEODORIDAS: Second half of the third century B.C. From Syracuse. He was known to have written both mock and genuine epitaphs, dedications, and a wide variety of other lyrics.

Finding List

Callimachus | A. W. Mair, ed. *Callimachus: Hymns and Epigrams.* Rev. ed. Loeb Classical Library. London: Heinemann, 1955.

Lobel and Page | Edgar Lobel and Denys Page. *Poetarum Lesbiorum Fragmenta.* Oxford: Clarendon Press, 1955.

Lyra Graeca | J. M. Edmonds, ed. *Lyra Graeca.* Rev. ed. 3 vols. Loeb Classical Library. London: Heinemann, 1928–40.

Paton | W. R. Paton, ed. *The Greek Anthology.* 5 vols. Loeb Classical Library. London: Heinemann, 1916–18.

Trypanis I | Constantine A. Trypanis, ed. *The Penguin Book of Greek Verse.* Harmondsworth: Penguin, 1971.

Trypanis II | Constantine A. Trypanis, ed. *Callimachus: Aetia, Iambi, Hecale.* Loeb Classical Library. London: Heinemann, 1958.

ALKAIOS
"Agriculture": *Lyra Graeca,* vol. I, p. 422, #167.
"Bacchus": *Lyra Graeca,* vol. I, p. 416, #158.
"Courage": *Lyra Graeca,* vol. I, p. 406, #137A and B.
"Drink, and Get Drunk with Me": Lobel and Page, section B, #6.

"Drinking": *Lyra Graeca,* vol. I, p. 420, #163.
"Frankness": *Lyra Graeca,* vol. I, p. 406, #140.
"Friendship": *Lyra Graeca,* vol. I, p. 406, #139.
"History": *Lyra Graeca,* vol. I, p. 378, #90.
"Love": Paton, vol. I, p. 132, #10.
"Mourning": *Lyra Graeca,* vol. I, p. 348, #42.
"Movers and Shakers": *Lyra Graeca,* vol. I, p. 408, #143.
"Parvenu": *Lyra Graeca,* vol. I, p. 408, #142.
"Patience": *Lyra Graeca,* vol. I, p. 420, #162.
"Philosophy": *Lyra Graeca,* vol. I, p. 426, #173.
"Piggery": *Lyra Graeca,* vol. I, p. 358, #62.
"Politics": *Lyra Graeca,* vol. I, p. 352, #50.
"Poverty": *Lyra Graeca,* vol. I, p. 332, #18.
"Social Relations": *Lyra Graeca,* vol. I, p. 364, #71.
"Sorrow": *Lyra Graeca,* vol. I, p. 402, #132.
"True Luxury": *Lyra Graeca,* vol. I, p. 416, #157.
"Truth": *Lyra Graeca,* vol. I, p. 398, #126.
"Wine": *Lyra Graeca,* vol. I, p. 424, #169.

ALKMAN
"Fate and Necessity": *Lyra Graeca,* vol. I, p. 127, #142.
"Gluttonous Alkman": *Lyra Graeca,* vol. I, p. 83, #46.
"Not Aphrodite, No": *Lyra Graeca,* vol. I, p. 73, #26.
"O Dancers": *Lyra Graeca,* vol. I, p. 73, #26.
"Set Seven Couches": *Lyra Graeca,* vol. I, p. 123, #138.
"Tantalus": *Lyra Graeca,* vol. I, p. 101, #89.
"The Peaks Are Asleep": *Lyra Graeca,* vol. I, p. 77, #36.
"Try Singing": *Lyra Graeca,* vol. I, p. 101, #87.

ANONYMOUS
"A Mirror": Paton, vol. V, p. 564, #56.
"An Epitaph": Paton, vol. II, p. 128, #224.
"An Oracle": Paton, vol. V, p. 66, #81.
"Aristo": Paton, vol. II, p. 294, #546.
"Earthquake": Paton, vol. III, p. 276, #501.
"Epigram": Paton, vol. IV, p. 94, #51.
"Epitaph": Paton, vol. II, p. 188, #350.
"Lovers' Dialogue": Paton, vol. I, p. 174, #101.

"Message to the Living": Paton, vol. II, p. 184, #342.
"Miracle": Paton, vol. II, p. 174, #324.
"On Being Old": Paton, vol. III, p. 70, #138.
"On Homer": Paton, vol. V, p. 340, #301.
"On Love": Paton, vol. I, p. 132, #11.
"Patriots": Paton, vol. III, p. 34, #65.
"Prayer": Paton, vol. IV, p. 56, #108.

ANTIPATER OF SIDON
"Alkmenes": Paton, vol. II, p. 98, #172.
"Amyntor": Paton, vol. II, p. 130, #232.
"Ares, God of War": Paton, vol. III, p. 174, #323.
"Diodorus": Paton, vol. II, p. 334, #625.

ANTIPATER OF THESSALONIKA
"A Quarrel": Paton, vol. III, p. 142, #269.
"Europa": Paton, vol. I, p. 178, #109.
"Poetic Gift": Paton, vol. III, p. 48, #93.

ANYTE
"Epitaph for a Slave": Paton, vol. II, p. 288, #538.
"Hermes": Paton, vol. III, p. 168, #314.
"Stranger": Paton, vol. V, p. 295, #228.
"Venus": Paton, vol. III, p. 74, #144.

ARATUS
"In the Beginning": Trypanis I, p. 308, #154.

ASCLEPIADES
"Dry Fruit": Paton, vol. II, p. 122, #217.
"Pythias": Paton, vol. I, p. 206, #164.
"Rendezvous": Paton, vol. I, p. 198, #150.

CALLIMACHUS
"An Epitaph": Paton, vol. II, p. 244, #447.
"Charidas": Paton, vol. II, p. 282, #524.
"Critas' Tomb": *Callimachus,* p. 146, #XIV.
"Grouse": *Callimachus,* p. 156, #XXX.

"My Hunter Love": *Callimachus,* p. 158, #XXXII.
"My Mind": Trypanis I, p. 310, #156.
"Stepmothers": *Callimachus,* p. 142, #VIII.
"The Statue of Apollo at Delos": Trypanis II, p. 88, #114.
"The Unknown's Tomb": Paton, vol. II, p. 152, #277.
"Winning and Losing": Paton, vol. III, p. 314, #566.

DIONYSIOS OF ANDROS
"An Epitaph": Paton, vol. II, p. 286, #533.

GLAUKOS
"Daphnis and Pan": Paton, vol. III, p. 184, #341.

HEGEMON
"Thermopylae": Paton, vol. II, p. 238, #436.

LEONIDAS
"On Clito": Paton, vol. I, p. 418, #226.

LEONIDAS OF TARENTUM
"An Epitaph": Paton, vol. II, p. 352, #660.
"His Own Epitaph": Trypanis I, p. 339, #181.
"The Vine and the Goat": Trypanis I, p. 338, #179.

MELEAGER
"Daphnis": Paton, vol. II, p. 288, #535.
"Heliodora": Paton, vol. I, p. 196, #143.
"On Himself": Paton, vol. II, p. 224, #417.
"Spring": Paton, vol. III, p. 196, #363.
"Timo": Paton, vol. I, p. 228, #204.
"To Venus": Paton, vol. I, p. 382, #162.

MENANDER
"The Source of Destruction": Trypanis I, p. 282, #141.
"Vanity": Trypanis I, p. 282, #140.

MENECRATES
"Old Age": Paton, vol. III, p. 28, #54.

PERSES
"On Pregnancy": Paton, vol. I, p. 444, #272.

PHALAECUS
"The Sea and the Land": Paton, vol. II, p. 346, #650.

PHILODEMUS
"A Girl's Speech": Paton, vol. I, p. 292, #306.
"Rendezvous": Paton, vol. I, p. 184, #120.

PHOCYLIDES
"The Lerians": Trypanis I, p. 156, #70.

PLATO
"A Cautionary Tale": Paton, vol. III, p. 24, #44.
"An Epitaph": Paton, vol. II, p. 146, #265.
"On Love": Paton, vol. I, p. 166, #80.
"The Eretrian Dead": Trypanis I, p. 276, #136.
"Time": Paton, vol. III, p. 28, #51.

POSIDIPPUS
"Party Preparations": Paton, vol. I, p. 218, #183.

SIMONIDES
"An Epitaph": Paton, vol. II, p. 142, #254A.
"Epitaph for a Workman": Paton, vol. II, p. 276, #507A.
"How to Tell": *Lyra Graeca,* vol. II, p. 333, #90.
"On His Spear": Paton, vol. I, p. 326, #52.
"Sailors": Paton, vol. II, p. 148, #270.
"The Defenders of Tegea": Trypanis I, p. 166, #86.
"Timon": Paton, vol. II, p. 187, #348.

TERPANDER
"Of Sparta": Lobel and Page, #941.
"To Apollo": *Lyra Graeca,* vol. 1, p. 31, #2.
"To Zeus": Lobel and Page, #698.

THEODORIDAS
"An Epitaph": Paton, vol. II, p. 154, #282.
"Euphorion": Paton, vol. II, p. 218, #406.

BURTON RAFFEL is distinguished professor emeritus of arts and humanities at the University of Louisiana at Lafayette. His many translations include Stendhal's *The Red and the Black,* for the Modern Library; Rabelais's *Gargantua and Pantagruel,* winner of the 1991 French-American Foundation Translation Prize; Chrétien de Troyes's five Arthurian romances; Cervantes's *Don Quijote;* Balzac's *Père Goriot;* and *Beowulf,* his version of which has sold more than a million copies.

A NOTE ON THE TYPE

The principal text of this Modern Library edition
was set in a digitized version of Janson, a typeface that
dates from about 1690 and was cut by Nicholas Kis,
a Hungarian working in Amsterdam. The original matrices have
survived and are held by the Stempel foundry in Germany.
Hermann Zapf redesigned some of the weights and sizes for
Stempel, basing his revisions on the original design.